Ways to Do
SURVEYS

Judith Anderson

A⁺

Smart Apple Media

This book has been published in cooperation with Franklin Watts.

Editor: Jennifer Schofield

Consultant: Steve Watts
(FRGS, Principal Lecturer University of Sunderland)

Art director: Jonathan Hair

Design: Mo Choy

Picture researcher: Kathy Lockley

Artwork: Ian Thompson

Acknowledgements:

Fred Bavendam/Still Pictures 40, John Birdsall Social Issues Photo Library 34–25,
B.S.P.I./CORBIS 6, Julio Etchart/Alamy Images 41, Eye Ubiquitous 30, Owen Franken/
CORBIS 19, Simon Fraser/Science Photo Library 9, Geogphotos/Alamy Images 25,
Sally & Richard Greenhill 38, Jeremy Horner /CORBIS 3b, 11, COVER, Hulton-Deutsch Collection/
CORBIS 32, Ton Koene/Still Pictures 43, Richard Levine/Alamy Images 7, K. Lockley 28,
Kimimasa Myama/Reuters/CORBIS 21, Richard T. Nowitz/CORBIS 15, PCL/Alamy Images 36,
Steve Sant/Alamy Images 27, Jorgen Schytte/Still Pictures 13, Dennis Scott/CORBIS 3T, 4–5, COVER
Stockbyte Platinum/Alamy Images 23, SuperStock/Alamy Images 31, Jochen Tack/Still Pictures 26,
Franklin Watts Archive 29, c. Janine Wiedel/Alamy Images 39, Courtesy of Winchester City Council 17

Published in the United States by Smart Apple Media

2140 Howard Drive West, North Mankato, Minnesota 56003

Printed in the United States

Library of Congress Cataloging-in-Publication Data

Anderson, Judith (Judith Mary)

Ways to do surveys / by Judith Anderson.

p. cm. — (Geography skills)

Includes index.

ISBN-13: 978-1-59920-053-8

1. Surveying—Juvenile literature. I. Title.

TA545.A548 2007

526.9—dc22   2006036140

9 8 7 6 5 4 3 2 1

Contents

What is a survey?

In geography, we ask ourselves questions all the time. What is the weather like? How long is that river? Why is there so much pollution? In order to find the answers, we collect the necessary information, record it, compare it, and interpret it. We make a survey.

Tourists interpret maps to be able to find their way around new cities.

6

HOW A SURVEY WORKS

Some surveys are very simple. For example, if you count the number of trees near your school, you are taking a survey. The number of trees is the result of your survey.

DATA

A survey is more than a random collection of information. It is usually information of a very specific kind, and is usually gathered in order to answer a particular question. This kind of information is called data. Data can be numbers, measurements, written information, or even opinions.

A street survey in New York. People are asked to give information about their habits and opinions.

HELPING HAND
Throughout this book, this helping hand will give you useful hints and tips.

WHAT DO YOU WANT TO KNOW?

We all need information in order to learn about our world. Imagine that you are going to travel to a country you know nothing about. What do you want to investigate before you get there? You may want to find out things such as:

- How big is it?
- What is the weather like?
- Do many people live there?
- What kind of food will I eat?

One way to learn more about a country is to look at maps or photographs. You might find a temperature chart on the Internet or read a travel book. When you have some information about this new country, you might compare it to what you already know about your own country. Is it hotter or colder? Is it more or less rural? Are there more people, or fewer?

By counting, measuring, observing, mapping, photographing, and seeking other people's opinions, we can begin to find some answers to questions about the varied and ever-changing world in which we live.

KEY SKILLS
Throughout this book, you will learn different skills. Each different skill is represented by one of the following icons:

 Completing a practical activity

 Analyzing and interpreting information

 Looking at graphs, maps, diagrams, and photographs

 Looking at global issues

 Researching information

 Observing

Starting out

Before beginning a survey, decide what you want to find out. Be as specific as possible. Perhaps you have been asked to carry out a weather survey. However, a weather survey can mean many things. Are you measuring rain? Are you keeping a log of weather conditions throughout a month? Are you trying to find out whether or not the weather affects people's weekend activities? Each question requires a different set of information.

DIFFERENT INFORMATION

If you are measuring rain, you will need a rain gauge, a pen, and some paper. However, if you are asking people for their habits or opinions, you may need to make a questionnaire. An investigation about the average weather conditions throughout a month would involve measuring rainfall, temperature, and several other types of data, too.

PLANNING

It is always a good idea to plan your survey carefully before you start. Not only do you need to know what you want to find out but also what tools to use and how to sort and present the results.

HELPING HAND
A computer database is a good way to store and sort a lot of factual information.

COLLECTING INFORMATION

Here are some tools that may help you collect information or data for your survey:

- paper and pen
- camera
- aerial photographs
- maps
- thermometer
- the Internet

Can you think of any others?

PRESENTING THE DATA

Once you have gathered your data, you will need to present your information. Here are some methods of sorting and presenting your results:

- graphs
- pie charts
- computer databases
- drawing maps
- written reports

Can you think of any others?

A meteorologist collects data from a rain gauge at Cape Grim, Australia.

⚠️ STAYING SAFE

Some of the surveys in this book can be done at school or at home. However, some require you to gather data in stores, on the street, or in the country and adult supervision may be required. When you see a warning triangle, check with a responsible adult before you undertake your investigation.

Traffic survey

Roads are busy at certain times of the day, even in some remote places. Heavy traffic can lead to bad traffic jams and long delays. Exhaust fumes cause pollution that damages the environment. Traffic surveys help people understand the problems and find solutions.

CONDUCT A TRAFFIC SURVEY

Find out what can be done to improve the flow of traffic on a busy local road. In order to do this, you need to conduct a traffic survey. Different types of vehicles may require different solutions, so you need to record the number of cars, trucks, vans, buses, and other vehicles. Do not forget to count bicycles! Before you start, make a form like this.

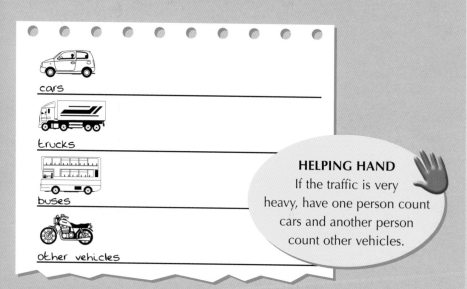

HELPING HAND
If the traffic is very heavy, have one person count cars and another person count other vehicles.

With a friend, watch the traffic on a busy local road for one hour. Make sure you are in a safe place with a clear view. Every time a vehicle goes by, put a check mark on the form showing what kind of vehicle it is. After an hour, discuss what you saw with your friend and make some notes. Was the traffic moving slowly or were some vehicles traveling too fast?

LOOK AT YOUR RESULTS

Count the number of check marks you have made for each type of vehicle. You might find it useful to make a bar graph similar to this one.

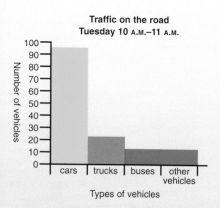

TRAFFIC CALMING

Heavy traffic can be dangerous, especially near a school or in a residential area. Decide which of the following would be most useful along the road you have surveyed:

- speed bumps: these are used to slow down cars and other vehicles.
- "No Parking" signs: these mean that the road is not blocked by parked vehicles.
- traffic lights: these regulate the flow of traffic at intersections and enable pedestrians to cross safely.
- road signs: these warn drivers to drive carefully.

Traffic often builds up during "rush hour" at the beginning and end of each day, when many people are traveling to and from work.

KEY SKILLS

Setting up a traffic survey

Observing and counting different vehicles

Analyzing and interpreting the survey results

Presenting data as a bar graph

The journey to school

Investigating how far children at your school travel each day can tell you a lot about the local community. It is useful if you are thinking about town planning, traffic congestion, or road safety.

GETTING STARTED

The first thing to consider is what kind of data you need and why. If you simply ask children to tell you how far they have traveled, you could end up with many different answers. Sometimes it is a good idea to group answers under suitable headings. For example, a form like the one below makes it easier for you to sort your data into meaningful results.

LOOK AT YOUR RESULTS

Once you have completed your survey, decide how you want to display your results. A bar graph is often the simplest method.

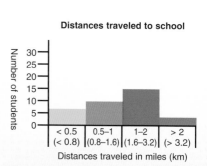

Distances traveled to school

Another method is to sketch a map of your school and the surrounding area. You could use a local map as a starting point. Draw your school at the center, and mark the distances by using a compass to draw circles radiating out from your school. Write the number of children traveling each distance on the appropriate circle. Make sure you display the scale you have used.

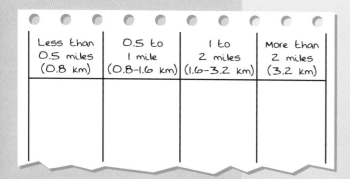

Less than 0.5 miles (0.8 km)	0.5 to 1 mile (0.8–1.6 km)	1 to 2 miles (1.6–3.2 km)	More than 2 miles (3.2 km)

HELPING HAND
If some children travel very long distances to school, you may want to include another column to show this.

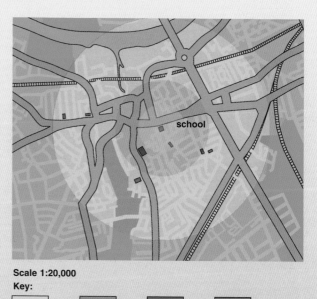

Scale 1:20,000
Key:

< 0.5 mi (< 0.8 km)	0.5–1 mile (0.8–1.6 km)	1–2 miles (1.6–3.2 km)	> 2 miles (> 3.2 km)

Some schools are in villages in sparsely
populated rural areas. Other schools are in urban
areas. Why might this affect the distance traveled by children to
school? Look at a map of your school and the surrounding area
and compare it with the map you sketched. Where are the main
residential areas? Is your school in a good location? Is there
another location that would be better?

*These children are on their
way to school in Zinder, Niger.
Some of them have walked
more than 3 miles (5 km).*

Shopping habits

Supermarket or convenience store? Department store or local shop? Stores come in many shapes and sizes. People often use large shopping malls and supermarkets for most of their shopping, but smaller, more local stores are still an important part of many communities.

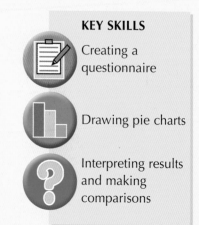
WHERE DO YOU SHOP?

Find out where people choose to shop for various items and if this has changed over the years. Making a questionnaire is a useful way to ask people about their habits or opinions. You will need to make a list of the questions you want to ask. You will also need to provide a range of possible answers from which people can choose. Offering a choice of possible answers makes it easier to display and interpret your results. Make a questionnaire like the one below.

	Newspaper	Bread	Shoes	TV	Vacation
Local stores					
Department stores					
Supermarkets					
Shopping malls					
Internet					

Try to ask about 20 adults who are at least 35 years old where they usually shop for certain items. Then ask them where they shopped for the same items 20 years ago. You could do this on a separate questionnaire or use the same questionnaire, but record their answers in a different color.

LOOK AT YOUR RESULTS

First, decide how you want to display the results—pie charts are a good way to make comparisons. Discuss your results with a friend. Do you notice any patterns of change over time? Why do you think such changes are taking place? Are these changes good or bad? Think about things such as transportation, convenience, and the impact on the environment.

This row of small shops is in the middle of a housing development on the edge of Australia's capital, Sydney.

DRAWING PIE CHARTS

If you have asked 20 people about their shopping habits, you will need to divide your pie chart into 20 equal segments. Then, to work out the proportions, color in the correct number of segments for each type of store.

Shopping for newspapers

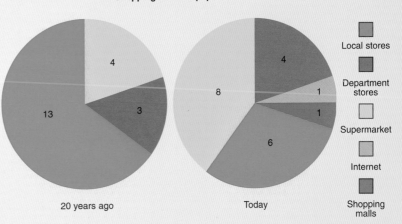

20 years ago

Today

Local stores

Department stores

Supermarket

Internet

Shopping malls

15

Collecting local opinions

Most of us have an opinion about where we live. Do we like it? Is it attractive? Are there enough stores, schools, or things to do? Is it convenient? Is it safe? Often people have very different opinions.

THE BIG ISSUE

The downtown area of many cities is busy during the week. People who drive to work or shop may not be able to find a parking space. To alleviate this problem, some cities build huge parking lots on the outskirts of cities where people can park their cars and take a bus into the city. This is called "park-and-ride."

DIVIDED OPINIONS

Winchester is an historic city in the UK. When the town planners decided to create a new park-and-ride program to reduce congestion and pollution in the city, they wanted to build it on some meadowland nearby. Local opinions were sharply divided about its location.

 WHAT IS YOUR VIEW?

Conduct a survey of local opinions on a possible park-and-ride program in your town. However, opinions can be difficult to measure. A useful way to collect opinions is to make a statement and then ask people whether they agree, do not know, or disagree.

	Agree	Do not know	Disagree
There are too many cars in the city			
A park-and-ride program is the best way to deal with traffic congestion			
I would use a park-and-ride program			

HELPING HAND
Make sure your statements are clear and easy to understand.

"The Council must realize that it cannot keep destroying the environment for the sake of traffic!"

"The park-and-ride program will help to reduce congestion and improve air quality in the city."

"Our traffic problems are having a bad effect on shops and businesses in our city!"

Users of this park-and-ride program leave their cars in a special parking lot, two miles (3.2 km) from downtown and complete their journey by bus.

YOUR RESULTS

A pie chart or a bar graph is a suitable way to display the results of each statement. What do your results show? People often agree that a problem exists. The difficulty comes with finding a solution. Can you think of any other ways to reduce the volume of traffic in a downtown area? How do other cities deal with the problem?

KEY SKILLS

 Collecting opinions to complete a survey

 Analyzing and interpreting information

 Making bar graphs or pie charts

 Looking at other cities, either local or international

Transporting food

What have you eaten today? Where has your food come from? Perhaps you grew it yourself. Perhaps some of it was bought in a supermarket. Most of our food has made a much longer journey than the one from supermarket to plate.

IMPORTING FOOD

Most kiwifruit are grown in New Zealand. Thirty years ago, few people in other parts of the world had seen a kiwifruit. Now they are available in almost every supermarket. Modern methods of storing, preserving, and transporting food mean that it lasts longer and can travel greater distances more cheaply. Stores are full of fruits, vegetables, and other goods from all over the world.

COUNTRY OF ORIGIN

Find out how far different types of food have traveled. Make a table like the one shown here—choose at least five different foods. Complete your survey by looking at the labels on food at home or by visiting a supermarket and making a list of all of the different countries where the food was grown or produced.

	COUNTRY OF ORIGIN
COFFEE	
BROCCOLI	
APPLE JUICE	
RICE	
BACON	
SUGAR	
ORANGES	

HELPING HAND
The place from which something comes is called its country of origin.

WHICH IS THE FARTHEST?

One way to display your results is to mark them on a map of the world. Give each food a different color and use colored pencils to draw a line from the country of origin to your home. Measure the distance according to the scale of the map. You could record your findings on a bar graph.

DIFFERENT OPINIONS

Some people feel that it is better to eat locally grown food as much as possible. This supports local farmers and means that there is less pollution caused by air travel. Other people welcome the availability of foods from around the world and enjoy eating foods that are out of season locally.

What do you think? Discuss your opinions with a friend. Consider things such as choice, convenience, and the impact on farmers, producers, and the environment.

Growers in the Windward Islands depend on the export of bananas overseas, but transporting produce around the world by land, sea, or air has a negative impact on the environment.

KEY SKILLS

Completing a table

Interpreting and analyzing results

Looking at food labels

Understanding global issues

International perspectives

Many of the surveys in this book are local surveys, investigating local sites and issues. However, some surveys involve collecting data from other cities, regions, or even other countries. When we cannot do the counting, measuring, photographing, or interviewing ourselves, we collect data from secondary sources such as the Internet.

INVESTIGATING A NATURAL DISASTER

Investigate a natural disaster such as an earthquake or a flood in another country. Find out why it happened, what it was like when it happened, and the problems faced by rescuers and survivors. What type of data is needed? Think about each of the following:

- maps
- weather reports
- statistics
- news reports
- aerial photographs
- interviews with local people

HELPING HAND
A TV news report will provide pictures and some information, but do not forget to use other sources, too.

Where might you find these different types of data? Why do you think you will need them?

EARTHQUAKE IN NORTHERN PAKISTAN

When an earthquake struck the mountainous areas of northern Pakistan and India in October 2005, nearly 100,000 people lost their lives. Many more people were injured or homeless. Rescuers had problems reaching the survivors. What do the following sources of information tell you about the situation?

"There are not enough precious helicopters to reach the more than 3 million survivors, so aid workers have now resorted to the painfully slow method of using mules to reach otherwise inaccessible villages before the snow arrives."

Source: Reuters November 7, 2005

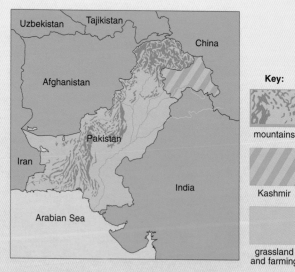

Key:

mountains

Kashmir

grassland and farming

Write a short report on the disaster using only the information provided here. What other types of data would help you create a more detailed survey of the problems faced by survivors?

A truck hit by falling rocks blocked the road to the mountain village of Divilain in Pakistani-controlled Kashmir in October 2005.

PLANNING FOR THE FUTURE

Some natural disasters, such as earthquakes and tsunamis, cannot be avoided. However, surveys of the region, its geography, and its people can provide valuable information about how to prepare for future disasters and limit their destructive power. What do you think could be done to save lives in the event of another earthquake in the region? Think about the following:

- housing
- transportation
- weather
- emergency supplies
- planning

KEY SKILLS

 Using secondary sources to gather information

 Looking at maps and photographs

 Writing a report

21

Improving disabled access

Public space means a place that is accessible to everyone. Parks, public libraries, museums, and shopping malls are all public spaces. However, any public space needs to be planned very carefully in order to ensure that people with disabilities can use it easily.

Can you think of any public spaces near you that may create difficulties for people with disabilities?

LOCAL LIBRARY

Make a survey of your local library. Find out whether anything can be done to improve disabled access. First, discuss with a friend the problems that disabled people might encounter. If possible, talk to wheelchair users, people with impaired sight or hearing, elderly people, and others. What do they think?

Now, make a table like the one below. Is there anything you want to add?

KEY SKILLS

Observing surroundings

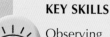
Completing a survey; writing a formal letter

Interpreting results

	YES	NO
Ramps for wheelchairs and motorized scooters		
Automatic doors		
Low information desk		
Easy-to-reach shelving		
Lift for wheelchairs		
Good lighting		

When you visit the library to make your observations and fill in your table, use a camera to make a visual record of what you see. Photographs can be very important data when making a survey of this kind.

HELPING HAND
When taking photographs, give an idea of scale. If you think a shelf is too high, show someone trying to reach it or take a measurement and write it on the back of the photograph.

WHAT CAN BE DONE?

Think carefully about the data and comments you have collected. Is there anything that can be done to improve disabled access? Use the results of your survey to write a letter to the local city council, explaining how access might be improved. Remember to be polite and use formal language. You could enclose the photographs as evidence for your findings.

Surveying a stream

Rivers and streams undergo many physical changes as they move from their source to the mouth. They may flow quickly along channels or sharp inclines. They may meander across a plain. They may be joined by other rivers or streams and sometimes may flood. Surveys help us understand these changes.

KEY SKILLS

Surveying a stream

Interpreting results

Plotting a river cross section; labeling a map

 MEASURING WIDTH AND DEPTH

Measure the width and depth of a nearby stream. It is important to choose the stream carefully. It must be shallow enough for you to walk across easily, or it needs to have a footbridge from which you can safely lower a yardstick. Remember that even shallow water can be dangerous if it is moving quickly.

WIDTH

First, measure the width by stretching a long waterproof tape measure from one side of the stream to the other. Anchor each end of the tape measure with sticks, or ask two friends to hold the ends for you. Take a reading from where the dry bank meets the flow of water and write it down.

DEPTH

Next, use a yardstick or depth pole to measure the depth of the stream from the bottom to the surface. Move across the stream, using the tape measure as a guide to keep you in a straight line. Take further depth readings at 10-inch (25 cm) intervals until you reach the other side. Ask a friend to write down the readings for you.

If possible, repeat your survey at two different points along the stream. You could also repeat these measurements at different times of year—summer and winter, for example.

HELPING HAND
In order to make sure your reading is as accurate as possible, pull the tape measure taut and keep it at right angles to the stream's edge.

PLOT A CROSS SECTION

The best way to display your results is to plot them on a graph similar to the one shown here. This will give you an accurate cross section of the part of the stream you have surveyed. If you measured the stream at more than one point or at different times of year, show the results on a series of graphs, marking the position of each on a map and recording any reasons for variations in width and depth.

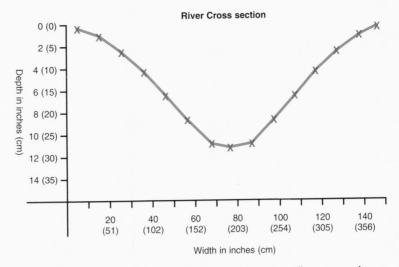

Observe what happens to the rate of water flowing along a stream when a channel suddenly narrows or widens. Can you think of any reasons why the shape of your stream may change over time?

The width and depth of a stream are being measured using a tape measure and a yardstick.

Using a river

People have always used rivers for water, food, and transportation. Look at a river on a map and you will see many cities clustered along its banks. Yet the ways in which people use rivers have changed over time and are continuing to change.

RIVER USE
Take a survey of river use. If possible, choose a local river. First, look at a map and decide on a suitable section of river for your survey. Two or three miles (4 km) may be enough.

A smelting factory at Duisberg, Germany beside the Rhine River.

MAKE A VISUAL SURVEY

Once you have decided which stretch of river to survey, sketch a simple map, making sure the scale is big enough to add words, drawings, and photographs as you collect your data.

⚠️ When visiting the section of river, record what you see beside the river, as well as the types of boats you see and activities taking place on it. Think about things such as transportation, drinking water, sewage, industry, farming, and recreation. Use a camera to take photographs of buildings and activities, and make drawings and notes on your map.

HELPING HAND
Make sure there is public access along the section of river you choose. You will need to be able to get to it!

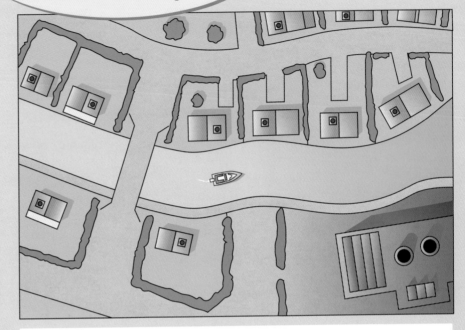

KEY SKILLS

 Using a map to find a river

 Observing a river

 Carrying out a survey; sketching maps

 Interpreting results

 Researching rivers around the world

INTERPRETING YOUR RESULTS

Is there any evidence for ways in which the river was used in the past? For example, are there docks that are no longer in use? What changes do you think may have occurred over time? What impact does the river have on the city today?

This former mill is now a tea shop for tourists.

For people in some parts of the world, river use may not have changed much throughout the past few hundred years. Research river use along the Amazon River in Brazil or the Ganges River in India and compare them to the river you have surveyed. What are the similarities? What are the differences?

Garbage at a glance

Dealing with garbage is a serious problem for every country in the world. In developed countries, such as the United States and Canada, each person generates an average of 1,100 pounds (500 kg) of garbage each year. Much of it is buried in landfill sites or burned, but this is very bad for the environment. However, before we can limit the amount of garbage we produce, we need to find out where it comes from.

WHAT IS IN YOUR GARBAGE?

Paper, food and garden waste, metals, glass, and plastics make up the bulk of most household garbage. However, examining the contents of your garbage can be a messy business. If you want to try, remember to wear gloves! A quick glance into the dumpsters in your school playground will probably be enough to show that much of our garbage comes from packaging.

WHAT IS IN YOUR LUNCHBOX?

Take a survey of packaging waste in school lunchboxes. However, measuring the waste in your school's garbage can may not be the best way to do this, because some children may take their garbage home with them. A more accurate method is to survey the contents of each lunchbox before the food is eaten.

Start by making a table like the one shown below. Then count the pieces of packaging, putting a check mark on the table next to each item. Do not forget to count fruit waste, too. An apple or banana would count as one item of fruit waste, because of the core or peel.

Fruit/vegetable waste (apple core, fruit peel, etc.)	
Plastic waste (snack wrapper, plastic bag, plastic utensils, etc.)	
Metal waste (soda pop can, etc.)	
Glass waste (drink bottle, etc.)	
Paper (napkin, bag, etc.)	

HELPING HAND
If you want your survey to be a true measure of lunchbox waste, don't tell anyone about it in advance!

REDUCE, REUSE, RECYCLE

After you have completed your first survey, tell everyone that there will be a second survey the next day and ask them to try to reduce the amount of packaging they bring. Food and drinks can be brought in reusable containers, for example. Then repeat your survey. How are you going to display your results?

Look at the contents of the lunchbox on page 28. How might the packaging be reduced? Is there any packaging that is completely unnecessary? What items could be reused? Is there anything in the lunchbox that could be recycled?

Tons of household garbage are dumped at landfill sites.

KEY SKILLS

Looking in garbage cans

Completing a survey

Interpreting and analyzing results

Water watch

Water is our planet's most valuable resource. We cannot live without it. The United Nations says that every person should have at least 13 gallons (50 l) of water per day for drinking, washing, cooking, and sanitation. In Europe, each person uses an average of 37 gallons (140 l) per day. However, people use as little as 2.6 gallons (10 l) in some less economically developed countries (LEDCs).

KEY SKILLS

 Looking at global issues

 Completing a survey; making lists

 Interpreting survey results

Researching information

Women and children collecting water from a village well in Rajasthan, India

DIFFERENCES IN WATER USAGE

There are many reasons for this difference in water usage. More economically developed countries (MEDCs) use a lot of water because pipes bring it directly into homes and people can afford to use dishwashers, garden hoses, toilets, and showers. In poorer LEDCs, people may have to walk to a well to collect water in containers they must carry themselves.

Can you think of any other reasons to explain why some countries use more water than others?

HOW MUCH DO YOU USE?

Take a survey to see how much water you use each day. Make a table like the one below and record each time you turn on a faucet or flush the toilet during a 24-hour period. Ask other members of your family to do the same.

Running a hose for 15 minutes can use as much as 66 gallons (250 l) of water.

Amount of water used	Number of times	Total
Bath 21 gallons (80 l)		
Shower 8 gallons (30 l)		
Flush the toilet 2 gallons (9 l)		
Wash hands		
Brush teeth		
Run tap for other reason		
Total amount of water used		

HELPING HAND
An easy way to measure the amount of water you use when you turn on a faucet is to allow 0.25 gallons (1 l) per 10 seconds. So if you run a faucet for 30 seconds to wash your hands, you have used 0.75 gallons (3 l) of water.

Of course, your household probably uses water in many other ways during the same 24-hour period. What about cooking and cleaning? Do you use a dishwasher or a washing machine? Do you have a yard that is watered with a sprinkler or a car that is washed using a hose?

Visit the water usage calculator at:
www.tampagov.net/dept_water/conservation_education/customers/water_use_calculator.asp
to find out how much water is used in your home. Compare your results with those of your friends. Whose home is the most wasteful? How could you reduce the amount of water used?

Forest habitats

Forests are a vital part of our planet's ecosystem. They provide food and shelter for many plants and animals. Without forests, our air and climate would be different, as well as the surface of the land that trees help to bind together. Nevertheless, the world's forest and woodland habitats are changing and some are disappearing altogether.

For years, logging has damaged forest habitats across the world. Today, many forests are carefully managed to protect the habitat and to minimize the damage we cause.

⚠ WOODLAND SURVEY

Take a general survey of a woodland habitat near you in order to learn about some of the issues that affect forests.

First, sketch a map of the area. You may prefer to draw your outline using local maps. Choose a suitable scale and remember to include physical features such as rivers or hills as well as roads, footpaths, and other evidence of human activity such as parking lots, coppiced areas, or trees that were cut for timber.

Now look at the types of trees in your area of woodland. If the trees are mainly evergreen, then it is a coniferous habitat. If the leaves on the trees are mainly broad-leaved and fall off during fall, then it is a deciduous habitat. If the trees are a mixture of the two, then it is a mixed woodland habitat.

Next, make a list of the different plants and animals in your chosen habitat. These include those you can actually see, those that leave evidence such as nests or droppings, and those that may be completely hidden from view but you know about them from guidebooks or wildlife experts. The different plants and animals make up the biodiversity of woodland habitats.

> **HELPING HAND**
> Food chains can be long or short but they usually start with plants and end with a predator.

FOOD CHAINS

This biodiversity can be displayed as a series of food chains.
For example:

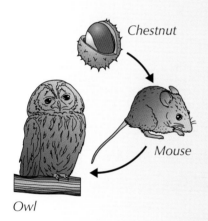

Chestnut

Mouse

Owl

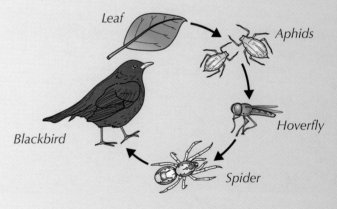

Leaf

Aphids

Hoverfly

Spider

Blackbird

What food chains can be made from your list of plants and animals?

KEY SKILLS

 Looking at forests

 Sketching maps; completing a survey; drawing food chains

 Interpreting results

CHANGE OVER TIME

Try to figure out if your area of woodland has changed over the last 20 years. Think about the impact of tourism, industry, and nearby housing. Does the woodland have "protected" status? Has any of it been lost because of new construction? Have any animals or plants disappeared, been introduced, or even reintroduced?

Weather watch

Weather is the condition of the air, or atmosphere, in a particular place at a particular time. It combines features such as temperature, humidity, air pressure, and precipitation. It is influenced by factors such as mountains and coasts, distance from the equator, and the seasons. The complex mix of these different elements can make weather difficult to predict. Meteorologists collect weather data to help them forecast conditions and also to see if weather patterns are changing over time.

SURVEYING THE WEATHER

Take a daily survey of cloud cover, temperature, and rainfall in your schoolyard over a single week. You will need to make a suitable chart for recording your information. Make sure you show dates and times as well as your observations and measurements.

WHAT CAN YOU SEE?

Choose a time each day to look at the sky and record what you see. The following abbreviations may be helpful:

- C – clear (no clouds)
- PC – partly cloudy (half cloudy/half clear)
- MC – mostly cloudy (cloudy with gaps)
- O – overcast (no clear sky at all)
- F – fog
- S – snow
- R – rain

HELPING HAND
Remember to collect your data at the same time each day.

AIR TEMPERATURE

Use a thermometer to measure the air temperature. Make sure your thermometer is in the shade and on fairly open ground. It may be attached to a wall or fence but not to the side of a building because this will distort the true temperature. If possible, use a thermometer that also shows minimum and maximum temperatures over a 24-hour period. Do not forget to reset it each day!

RAINFALL

Measure rainfall by using a ruler to see how much rain collects in a can or a bucket in a 24-hour period. If you prefer, you can use a simple rain gauge set in open ground for a more accurate reading. If the temperature is high, use a covered rain gauge to prevent water from evaporating.

SHARE INFORMATION

Ask students from a school in a different part of the country to take an identical survey during the same week. Use e-mail to share your data. Look at the location of both schools on a map that shows physical features such as coasts and mountains. What do you think causes the variations in the weather patterns?

KEY SKILLS
Using rain gauges and thermometers

Exchanging and comparing data by e-mail

Interpreting information

If you were keeping a record of cloud cover, this sky would be called "mostly cloudy."

Investigating climates

Climate is not the same as weather. Weather refers to conditions that are local and temporary. Climate, on the other hand, is about averages over time. For example, we know that a desert climate is dry, even though it may occasionally get rain.

Many ski resorts such as Davos, Switzerland are surrounded by alpine forests and high mountain peaks.

WILL THERE BE SNOW?

Investigate the climate of Davos, a busy winter ski resort in the Swiss Alps. First, use a map to examine the main features of the European mainland such as mountain ranges and coasts. Then, use a physical map of Switzerland to locate Davos. What is its altitude (height above sea level)? What are the main features of the area?

Look at these two graphs:

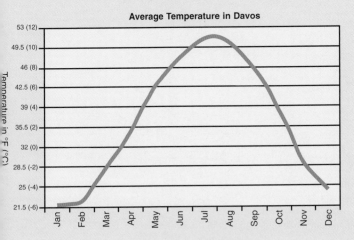

Average Temperature in Davos

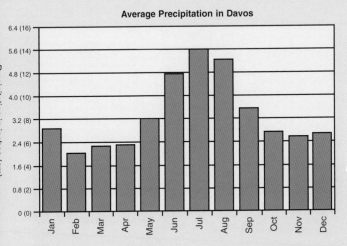

Average Precipitation in Davos

Using this information, describe why you think the climate in Davos is suitable for winter sports.

HOW MUCH DO WE KNOW?

During the winter months, skiers and snowboarders visit Davos because they know that the mountain slopes will be covered with snow. However, variations in local weather conditions may produce an unexpectedly heavy snowfall or dangerously high winds. Global warming may be contributing to a gradual change in climate, with milder, shorter winters and a loss of snow. Meteorologists continue to study weather and climate because both may be less predictable than they seem.

HELPING HAND
Global warming is an increase in the earth's temperature that may be caused by human activities such as burning oil, coal, and gas.

The dominant local issue in this Swiss ski resort is the freakish weather—spring-like temperatures that extended into the first days of January, with no snow below 6,500 feet (2,000 m). Few people living in Europe's lower-lying ski resorts need any convincing that their economy is being seriously affected by climate change.

Claude Martin, *International Herald Tribune,* January 23, 2003

Use the Internet to investigate the average snowfall and temperature patterns in the Swiss Alps throughout the past 20 years. Has the climate changed during this time?

KEY SKILLS

 Looking at Davos, Switzerland

 Interpreting maps and graphs

 Using the Internet

 Interpreting results

Entitlement expense

How do you spend your time? Most of us divide our day among work or school, sleep, and entertainment. However, entertainment means different things to different people. For some people, shopping and traveling are entertaining. For others, they are work. Looking at how people spend their free time can tell us a great deal about different lifestyles, communities, and the impact we have on our environment.

ENTERTAINMENT SURVEY

Investigate how you spend your free time. First, make a list of all the things you have done over the past week. Then try to group them into a maximum of ten different activities. For example, if you travel by car to school and to extracurricular activities, group this under car trips. If you visit different friends' houses, group this under friends or playing. The following chart is a guide, but yours may be different.

Record how long you spend on each activity daily. Remember that a day is 24 hours and there are 168 hours in a week. Then add up the figures for each activity to give you a weekly total.

	MON	TUES	WED	THU	FRI	SAT	SUN	total
Sleep								
School								
Mealtimes								
Car or bus trips								
Sport								
Playing (alone or with friends)								
Watching TV								
Reading								
Computer games								
Other activities/hobbies (shopping, going to the movies, going to the park)								

How has the demand for entertainment, such as going to the movies, affected your area?

CALCULATING AVERAGES

When you have added up your total amount of time for each activity, round it up or down to the nearest hour. Then calculate the average amount of time spent on this activity each day by dividing the total by 7 (the number of days in the week). Now display your results for your average day on a pie chart or a bar graph.

You can calculate the percentage of your average day spent on each activity by dividing your average by 24 and multiplying the answer by 100. How much of your day is spent on entertainment? Are you surprised by your results?

DIFFERENCES AROUND THE WORLD

Use the Internet to research how children in LEDCs might spend their day. How much free time do they have? What reasons explain the differences between your day and theirs?

Playing basketball in the park. Does the weather have an impact on how you spend your free time?

KEY SKILLS

Completing a survey

Using the Internet

Interpreting results

Making global comparisons

Tourism

Tourism is one of the world's fastest growing industries. The increased wealth of more economically developed countries has given people a greater amount of free time and money to take more vacations to destinations around the world.

KEY SKILLS
Sketching a map; completing questionnaires; writing an advertisement

Interpreting results

The natural wonders of the Great Barrier Reef off the coast of Australia attract large numbers of tourists, but conservationists are worried about the effect this has on a unique ecosystem.

TOURISTS AND TOURISM

Make sure you are familiar with the following terms. A *tourist* is someone who travels to a particular location for recreation. Their trip might be local or it might involve traveling long distances. A *tourist attraction* is a place, building, or event that many tourists visit. Museums, festivals, theme parks, and beaches are all examples of tourist attractions. *Tourism* is the business of supplying tourists' needs such as food, hotels, and transportation.

FIND THE ATTRACTION

Investigate a tourist attraction near you to determine who visits it and why.

First, decide on a suitable tourist attraction that you can visit easily. Sketch a map of the site and label its main features. How large is the site? Is it in the country or is it in a town? Do tourists have to pay to visit it? What transportation facilities are close by? Is there a parking lot?

Disney World employs 55,000 people at its 47-square-mile (122 sq km) site in Florida.

QUESTIONS FOR TOURISTS

Now create a questionnaire for tourists in order to find out what they like about the attraction and how far they have traveled. You may want to include the following questions:

- How far have you traveled?
- How did you travel?
- How long did you stay here?
- Would you come again or recommend it to others?
- What is the best thing about this attraction?
- What is the worst thing about this attraction?

Using the information you have collected, discuss with a friend whether your tourist attraction interests mainly local, regional, national, or international tourists. Is there anything that could be done to attract more visitors? Write a short advertisement for your chosen site. You can use persuasive language, but remember to stick to the facts.

PROBLEMS WITH TOURISM

Tourist attractions are often very important to local communities because they provide jobs and help create wealth. However, they can create problems, too. Sometimes the attraction itself damages the local wildlife habitat or causes pollution. More tourists mean more airplanes, buses, and cars, and more hotels, restaurants, and stores. What impact has your tourist attraction had on the local environment? Which do you think is more important—the benefits it brings, or the problems it creates?

A growing population

The world's population is growing fast. Estimates suggest that 4.4 people are born every second, while only 1.78 die. This rapid rise in population has a huge impact on the world's resources and our ability to manage them.

(RIGHT) These children in Africa are suffering from malnutrition; they do not have enough to eat. Why do you think Africa's infant mortality rate is nearly15 times higher than that of MEDCs?

DIFFERENCES AROUND THE WORLD

The global population may be growing, but population statistics, or demographics, vary hugely from country to country. In some countries, mainly MEDCs, the birthrate is slowing down while greater numbers of people are living longer than they did in the past. In other countries, mainly LEDCs, the birthrate is rising fast, but high infant mortality rates and shorter life expectancy may mean that fewer people are living into old age.

Disease, poverty, and migration are three factors that affect the population of individual countries. Can you think of other factors?

KEY SKILLS

Interpreting population pyramids

Using the Internet

Comparing countries around the world

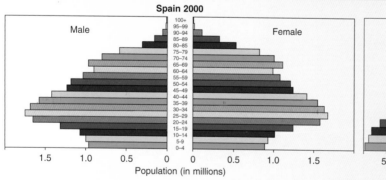

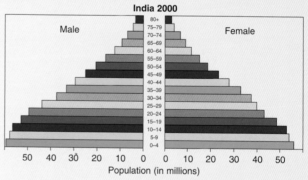

POPULATION PYRAMIDS

A population pyramid is a horizontal bar graph showing the age and sex ratios of a country's population. It can tell us a lot about the current population, as well as provide data for predicting what may happen in the future. Look at these two population pyramids.

The overall shape of each pyramid is very different. What do they tell you about the populations of Spain and India? Try to think of at least three things. Now look at the population pyramids for the same countries as predicted for the year 2050. What has changed?

Spain 2050

Male | Female

Population (in millions)
1.5   1.0   0.5   0   0   0.5   1.0   1.5

India 2050

Male | Female

Population (in millions)
50   40   30   20   10   0   0   10   20   30   40   50

Why do you think these changes have been predicted?
What impact are the changes likely to have on both countries?
Use the Internet to compare two more population pyramids:
that of your own country and that of an LEDC such as Uganda.
Are they very different? If so, why?

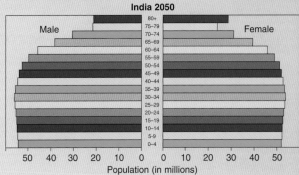

HELPING HAND
The U.S. Census Bureau
Web site (see page 45) provides
population pyramids for every
country in the world.

Glossary

Accessible
Something that everyone can enter or use without difficulty.

Atmosphere
The mixture of gases that surrounds the earth.

Biodiversity
The variety of plants and animals found within a particular habitat.

Birthrate
The rate at which people are born.

Climate
The average weather conditions of a certain area.

Climate change
A general change in climate that may be due to natural causes or the effects of pollution and global warming.

Computer database
A collection of data that is stored so that it can be accessed by computers.

Coppiced areas
Areas of woodland in which trees have been cut back to ground level to encourage vigorous regrowth.

Ecosystem
The combination of living things and their environment.

Food chain
A series of plants and animals, where each serves as food for the one above in the series.

Global warming
A gradual increase in the average temperature of the earth's atmosphere.

Habitat
The environment to which a plant or an animal is best suited and where it usually grows or lives.

Humidity
The level of moisture found in the atmosphere.

Less economically developed country (LEDC)
A country in which the majority of the population lives in poverty. These countries tend to be mainly rural, but their towns and cities are often growing fast.

Meteorologist
Someone who studies weather patterns and climate.

Migration
When people move from one region or area to another.

More economically developed country (MEDC)
A country with much greater wealth per person and more developed industry than a less economically developed country.

Mortality rate
The rate at which people die.

Population pyramid
A horizontal bar graph that shows the male and female populations of a country by age.

Precipitation
Water that falls from the atmosphere to the earth's surface, including rain, sleet, snow, and hail.

Recycle
To collect useful materials, such as glass and paper, and reprocess them into something else so that they can be used again.

Rural
In the country.

Scale
A system of numbering used on maps where one unit on the map represents a number of the same units on the ground. For example, a scale of 1:20,000 means that one unit on the map represents 20,000 of the same unit on the ground.

Secondary sources
Information from a secondhand source such as a newspaper or the Internet.

Settlements
Places where people live.

United Nations
An organization of countries from all over the world, created to promote peace and human rights.

Urban
In towns and cities.

Weather
The state of the atmosphere at a particular time and place. Weather includes the temperature, humidity, wind speed, and precipitation.

Web sites

www.geography.about.com
In addition to fascinating facts about geography, this site contains links to maps around the world, a geography glossary, and answers to frequently asked questions.

www.epa.gov
Official Web site of the U.S. Environmental Protection Agency with up-to-date environmental news and useful information on acid rain, climate change, water treatment, and more.

www.census.gov/ipc/www/idbpyr.html
Site maintained by the U.S. Census Bureau that provides current and predicted population pyramids for every country in the world.

www.worldclimate.com
Find climate information, such as the average maximum temperature and the average rainfall, for more than 85,000 cities around the world.

http://magma.nationalgeographic.com/ngexplorer/0309/quickflicks/
Watch a short movie about food chains and learn how all animals and plants play an important role in food chains.

www.earth911.org
Contains valuable information about recycling with up-to-date environmental news links; also includes a search for local recycling programs.

Note to parents and teachers:

Every effort has been made to ensure that these Web sites are suitable for children, that they are of the highest educational value, and that they contain no inappropriate or offensive material. However, because of the nature of the Internet, it is impossible to guarantee that the contents of these sites will not be altered. We strongly advise that Internet access be supervised by a responsible adult.

Index